INTRODUCTION

S0-BBC-191

I own nearly 20 books with motivational and/or instructional quotes and quotations. Prior to last season, I was reading one of these books when it occurred to me that it would be a good idea to have such a book for coaches and specifically, baseball coaches. I constantly use quotes and quotations with my players and have spent hundreds of hours digging for appropriate ones to use. Now there is a source for baseball coaches and players to use at their fingertips with over 300 entries.

In compiling the quotes/quotations used in this book, I researched my book shelves and my files that I have accumulated over the past 30 years. In addition, I contacted over 100 of my college baseball coaching colleagues for their input and received replies from almost 40 (see acknowledgments).

The book contains motivational quotes as well as "instructions" for coaches and players. Regarding motivation, William Warren in his book entitled, *Coaching and Motivation* (1983), put forth two definitions of motivation for coaches and players that uniquely fit the requirements for athletic competition. For coaches, Warren defined motivation as "a means of finding ways to get players to do things they might not want to do on their own." For players, he defined motivation as "having reasons for acting or failing to act." Warren's book is must reading for any coach looking for proven means to motivate their athletes.

I am a baseball coach and this book is written for baseball coaches at all levels of the game. Before proceeding, I would like to include here what a baseball coach is. The following was written by Dave Keilitz, Executive Director of the American Baseball Coaches Association (ABCA), on the occasion of the opening ceremony for the ABCA Hall of Fame's new exhibition now housed in the Louisville Slugger Museum in Louisville, Kentucky.

WHAT IS A BASEBALL COACH?

- he is a counselor, mentor, guardian and role model. . .
- he is also a groundskeeper, cheerleader, fund-raiser, communicator, and motivator. . .
- he is loyal and dedicated to his program, trusting and believing in those he works with. . .
- he is a master of the basics, knows and understands the sport and presents it with a positive attitude and unlimited enthusiasm; he is a doer but also a dreamer. . .
- he possesses integrity and courage and has an unbounded work ethic; he is a winner. . .
- but most of all he is a teacher and a leader who constantly strives to make his players and those around him better people. . .
- and finally, he is a person that believes in what he is doing, has a passion for the game and respects and appreciates his job because he knows that COACHING is the greatest and most rewarding profession in the world.

Finally, I wish to distinguish between a quote and quotation. A quote is a short comment or statement that has been often repeated without knowledge of who the original author was. I feel confident you will recognize many of those contained herein.

Quotations, on the other hand, are a word for word acknowledgment of what a known author has said either in print or in a clinic presentation where I was present. Some of the quotations you will recognize are not authored by baseball coaches. However, it is my belief that it is unwise to narrow the scope of powerful quotations to just baseball coaches. There are countless valuable quotations that are universally acceptable by all sports and many from authors who were not specifically referring to sport when they penned their gems.

It is my hope and prayer that you will use the contents of this book not only to help you in your coaching, but to help you be the inspiration and model that your players desperately need. In so doing, I further hope, as a result of your influence, that your players become the best they possibly can be on the field, but more importantly, that they develop the attitude, character, and integrity that will truly make them a success in life.

Dave Altopp

TABLE OF CONTENTS

ACKNOWLEDGMENTS

This project is by no means a one-man job. I am indebted to the innumerable baseball coaches and players who were quoted at the right time when someone had a pen in hand. I am just one coach whose life and teaching has been impacted by the printed word.

I am especially indebted to my many friends who took the time to submit one or more of the gems found in this book. I would like to thank them personally by listing their names here along with their current position, though many of them are now retired:

♦♦♦

Bill Arce, Claremont-Mudd College
Brad Bass, Wayland Baptist University
Bob Bennett, Fresno State University
Scott Berry, Mayville State University
Richard Case, Former Executive Director, USA Baseball

Bubba Cates, University of Tennessee - Martin
Bud Daniel, Retired, University of Wyoming
Danny Davis, University of North Carolina - Pembroke

Jim Dimick, Retired, St. Olaf College

"Dutch" Fehring, Retired, Stanford University

Larry Giangrasso, Central Alabama Community College

Gordie Gillespie, Ripon College

Charlie Greene, Retired, Miami Dade South Community College

John Herbold, California State University at Los Angeles

Woody Hunt, Cumberland University

Dewey Kalmer, Bradley University

Kirk Kelley, Lyon College

Jerry Kindall, Retired, University of Arizona

Elmer Kosub, Retired, St. Mary's University

Carroll Land, Retired, Point Loma Nazarene University

Danny Litwiler, Retired, Michigan State University

Manny Mantrana, St. Thomas University

Tim Mead, Walsh University

Clyde Miller, Gardner-Webb University

Ron Oestrike, Retired, Eastern Michigan University

Tom Petroff, Retired, University of Northern Colorado

Jim Pizzolatto, Nicholls State University

Gary Pullins, Retired, Brigham Young University

Bobby Randall, University of Kansas

Bob Riesener, University of Montevallo

Craig Rutter, Defiance College

Paul Sanagorski, Kansas Newman University

Jack Stallings, Retired, Georgia Southern University

Ike Tomlinson, Retired, Arkansas State University

Glen Tuckett, Retired, Brigham Young University

Finally, I want to thank my wife, Phyllis, who for 34 years has stood behind me through wins, losses, rain-outs, and changing jobs. She is the one person who has truly supported and allowed me to pursue my love affair with baseball because my priorities were in order: God, family, and then baseball.

FOR THE COACH

*"The way a team plays as a whole determines its success.
You may have the greatest bunch of individual stars in the world,
but if they don't play together, the club won't be worth a dime."*

BABE RUTH

A baseball coach is like a stagecoach.
He can't move without horses.
PETE ROSE

Ability will enable a man to go to the top,
but it takes character to keep him there.
JOHN WOODEN

About the only problem with success is that
it does not teach you how to deal with failure.
TOMMY LASORDA

A coach is in a powerful position with his players.
He should never abuse that power.

GORDIE GILLESPIE

A coach is mistaken if he thinks he doesn't
have to motivate his players.

GEORGE ALLEN

A coach should help players increase their self-esteem, not decrease it.
A coach who is not in charge of his players cannot run his team.

BRANCH RICKEY

A GOOD TEAM LEADER IS ONE WHO TAKES A LITTLE MORE THAN HIS SHARE OF THE BLAME AND A LITTLE LESS THAN HIS SHARE OF THE CREDIT. A GREAT MANAGER HAS A KNACK FOR MAKING PLAYERS THINK THEY ARE BETTER THAN THEY THINK THEY ARE.

Reggie Jackson

A leader has been defined as one who knows the way,
goes the way, and shows the way.

Al Figone in *Teaching the Mental Aspects of Baseball* (1991) identified four factors considered necessary for success in coaching baseball. They are:
1. The knowledge and application of the technical skills of the game.
2. Managerial or administrative skills (planning, organizing, directing, staffing).
3. Interpersonal or human skills.
4. Communication or motivating skills.

A life isn't significant except for its impact on other lives.
JACKIE ROBINSON

A man can make mistakes, but he isn't a failure
until he starts blaming someone else.
SAM RUTIGLIANO

Any criticism I make of anyone on my team,
I make because they are not performing up to their full potential.
VINCE LOMBARDI

A successful team beats with one heart.
A team should be an extension of the coach's personality.
AL MCGUIRE

A team without goals is just another ineffective committee.
Attack home plate all the time.
GORDIE GILLESPIE

Attitude is the criterion for success, but it can't be bought for a million dollars. Attitudes are simply not for sale.

DENIS WAITLEY

A winning attitude starts at the top of the organization.

PETE ROSE

Baseball always has been and always will be a game demanding team play.

BABE RUTH

Become a possibilitarian. No matter how dark things seem to be or actually are, raise your sights and see possibilities because they are *always* there.

NORMAN VINCENT PEALE

Be more concerned with your character than your reputation, because your character is what you really are. Your reputation is merely what others think you are.

JOHN WOODEN

Coaches don't win games. They prepare players to win games.

DICK WILLIAMS

Coaches who can outline plays on a blackboard are a dime a dozen.
The ones who win get inside their players and motivate.

Coaching is a profession of love.
You can't coach people unless you love them.
EDDIE ROBINSON

Coming together is a beginning, staying together is progress,
and working together is success.
HENRY FORD

Common sense is not really all that common.

Contentment is not getting what we want,
but rather being satisfied with what we have.

Do not follow where the path may lead.
Go instead where there is no path and leave a trail
VINCE LOMBARDI

Don't judge those who try and fail. Judge only those who fail to try.

Don't save a pitcher for tomorrow. It might rain.
LEO DUROCHER

Every day is a new opportunity. You can build on yesterday's success or put its failures behind and start over again. That's the way life is, with a new game everyday. And that's the way baseball is.
BOB FELLER

Failing to prepare is preparing to fail.
JOHN WOODEN

God gave us two ends to use: one to think with, the other to sit with.
Success depends on which you choose: heads you win, tails you'll lose.

He has the right to criticize who has the heart to help.
ABRAHAM LINCOLN

He who spends some time on his knees
has no trouble standing on his feet.

How hard is hitting? You ever walk into a pitch-black room full of furniture that you've never been in before and try to walk through it without bumping into anything? Well, hitting is harder than that.
TED KLUSZEWSKI

Humor is a great lubricant for teamwork.

I don't know the key to success,
but the key to failure is trying to please everybody.
BILL COSBY

If you are successful, you will win some false friends
and make some true enemies. Succeed anyway.

If you ignore it, that means you have accepted it.
RON OESTRIKE

If you play for me, you play the game like you play life. You play it to be successful, you play it with dignity, you play it with pride, you play it aggressively, and you play it as well as you possibly can.

BILLY MARTIN

I have long believed that pitching is notoriously under coached, that kids are taught to throw as hard as they can being obsessed with radar speeds rather than learning what makes their ball move from one side of the plate to the other and how to improve their control.

SKIP BERTMAN

I have seen many players with potential who didn't go anywhere.
They didn't want it badly enough. They didn't want to sacrifice.
It comes down to one word - dedication.

SPARKY ANDERSON

I have never seen a monument erected to a pessimist.

PAUL HARVEY

I judge a player by what he does for his team
and not by what he does for himself.

BILLY MARTIN

I NEVER QUESTIONED THE INTEGRITY OF AN UMPIRE. THEIR EYESIGHT, YES!
Leo Durocher

I PLAY MY BEST NINE NOT MY NINE BEST.
Skip Bertman

IT'S NOT WHAT YOU TELL YOUR PLAYERS THAT COUNTS. IT'S WHAT THEY HEAR.
Red Auerbach

In one of the most outstanding presentations at an American Baseball Coaches Association convention, John Scolinos outlined seven personalities of baseball players that the successful coach must be able to recognize and deal with. He warned that for a coach to last in this profession, he must know how to handle the "7 Balls of Baseball."

1. The Odd Ball - he's just different from the rest
2. The Snot Ball - cries all the time
3. Pus Ball - has no stability
4. Jerk Ball - is only concerned with himself, his numbers
5. Screw Ball - he doubts your ability as coach. Be careful of him because his doubts can spread to the rest of the team
6. Donk Ball - this is the donkey! The guy who will destroy your team. Get rid of him!
7. Hard Ball - the mentally tough guy; the guy who can adjust; he has a great attitude and the three C's: class, character, and concern. You want all your players to be like this.

Judge your success by what you had to give up to get it.

It's no fun throwing fastballs to guys who can't hit them.
The real challenge is getting them out on stuff they can hit.

SAM MCDOWELL

It takes the hammer of practice to drive the nail of success.

I was not interested in getting the best players available for my team. I
wanted the best players that fit into my program.

VINCE LOMBARDI

I would be the laughingstock of the league if I took the best left-handed pitcher in the league and put him in the outfield.

RED SOX MANAGER ED BARROW IN 1918

(ON MOVING BABE RUTH FROM THE MOUND TO A FULL-TIME POSITION)

Knowing and understanding the general personality of each player's ability to accept criticism is an essential of coaching.

NORM WILHELMI

Lord, help me to remember that nothing is going to happen to me today that You and I can't handle.

Make your practices like games. Make your games like practices.
JOHN HERBOLD

Maintaining the right attitude is easier than regaining the right attitude.

Most coaches think winning creates chemistry.
I think chemistry creates winning.
SPARKY ANDERSON

Most one-run games are lost, not won.
GENE MAUCH

My coach gave me the greatest gift anyone can give. He believed in me.
HOWARD TWILLEY

My goal as a coach is to set a standard higher than the players believe themselves capable of achieving - and then show them how to reach it.
LOU HOLTZ

My number one rule was "be on time."
If the players were not 10 minutes early, then they were late.
BOBBY WINKLES

Never concede a base to your opponent under any circumstances.
GORDIE GILLESPIE

NEVER LET AN INDIVIDUAL DOMINATE A TEAM.

No coach ever won a game by what he knows;
it is what his players have learned that wins.

Nothing is as hard as it looks,
everything is more rewarding than you expect,
and if anything can go right it will and at the best possible moment.

JOHN MAXWELL

OF ALL THE THINGS YOU WEAR,

YOUR EXPRESSION IS THE MOST IMPORTANT.

Once you find a job in baseball that you love,
you'll never work another day in your life.
DICK CASE

ONLY FOOLS MAKE PERMANENT DECISIONS WITHOUT

KNOWLEDGE OF ALL THE FACTS.

Open your arms to change, but don't let go of your values.

Our motto is **PRIDE**.

Personal

Responsibility

In

Developing

Excellence

BOB RIESENER

24

People catch our spirit just like they catch our colds:
by getting close to us.

People don't care how much you know
until they know how much you care.
JOHN MAXWELL

Players may swing the bat the same and have the same speed,
but they're different! You have to recognize you're dealing
with different personalities.
JIM LEYLAND

Praise loudly and blame softly.

Pray. There's immeasurable power in it.

Prefer the errors of enthusiasm to the complacency of wisdom.

BRANCH RICKEY

Remember coaches, you're not coaching baseball.
You are coaching people.

BILL ARCE

Remember not getting what you want is sometimes a stroke of luck.

Scold him, find fault with him and he could not pitch at all.
Praise him and he was unbeatable.
**FORMER CHICAGO MANAGER CAP ANSON ON HALL OF FAME PITCHER,
"SENSITIVE JOHN" CLARKSON**

Set your priorities. God is first, family is second,
team is third, I am fourth - and blessings will flow.
DAVE ALTOPP

Share your knowledge. It's a way to achieve immortality.

SILENCE CANNOT BE MISQUOTED.

Sometimes God may use defeat to remind you
where your abilities come from.

DOUG TEWELL

Sports and other forms of vigorous physical activity provide educational
experiences which cannot be duplicated in the classroom. They are an
uncompromising laboratory in which we must think and act quickly and
efficiently under pressure, and they force us to meet our own inadequa-
cies face to face . . . . as nothing else does.

BYRON WHITE (U.S. SUPREME COURT JUSTICE)

SUCCESSFUL TEAMS ARE BUILT ON THE STRENGTHS OF INDIVIDUAL MEMBERS.

Success is having the courage to meet failure without being defeated.
Although I cannot always control what happens to me,
I can control how I respond.

PHIL NIEKRO

Success is not determined by money or the things money can buy. It is
not determined by trophies on the shelf or by the letters after one's name.
Success is determined by one thing and one thing only:
when you leave this earth, is it better because you were here?

JIM DIMICK

Sure you feel better and you sleep better when you win, but there's nothing you can do about a game once it is over. You can't change it. You can replay it as many times as you want, but the score is always the same. All you can do is learn from it and look ahead to tomorrow.

WALT ALSTON

Surround yourself with good people. If you surround yourself with donkeys, they'll lead you to Donkeyville.

JOHN SCOLINOS

SYD THRIFT'S (FORMER PIRATES/YANKEES GENERAL MANAGER)
CHECKLIST FOR AN ACCURATE EVALUATION OF A <u>WHOLE BALLPLAYER:</u>

1. How great is the player's desire to excel?
2. How strong is his competitive spirit?
3. How aggressive is he?
4. How developed are his baseball instincts?
5. How does he react to adversity?
6. Can he make adjustments, physically and emotionally?
7. How great is his aptitude for baseball instruction?

TACT IS THE ART OF MAKING A POINT WITHOUT MAKING AN ENEMY.

Talent alone will only take a player so far. A positive attitude toward learning is one component that coaches must instill in players in order for them to ever develop whatever talent they may possess.

NORM WILHELMI

Talk slowly, but think quickly.

Teaching players WHAT to do is important, and teaching them HOW to do it is more important, but teaching them WHY to do it is the most important thing of all.

JACK STALLINGS

T.E.A.M.

TOGETHER EVERYONE ACHIEVES MORE

Team spirit is a competitive advantage.

The achievements of a team are the result
of the combined efforts of each individual team member.

VINCE LOMBARDI

The atmosphere you permit decides the attitude you convey.

The best coach is the coach that treats
every player as he would want his own son to be treated.

The best eraser in the world is a good night's sleep.

The best team doesn't win nearly as often as the team that gets along best
RON GILBERT

The coach is the team, and the team is the coach. They reflect each other.
SPARKY ANDERSON

The dictionary is the only place that success comes before work.
VINCE LOMBARDI

THE FIRST STEP TOWARD SUCCESS IS THE WILLINGNESS TO LISTEN.

The game isn't over till it's over.
YOGI BERRA

The greatest disservice you can do to your team
is to allow them not to respect the opposition.
LOU HOLTZ

The greatest need for player motivation is in practice sessions, because
practice makes permanent and how players practice is usually how they play.
JACK STALLINGS

The hardest thing to do in practice or a game is not make a big thing out
of everything. Make a big thing out of the big things!
ED CHEFF

The head coach should involve his assistants in making decisions though he alone must accept responsibility for the results.

The key to baseball skill development is *working hard on specific things in practice* rather than "just working hard" in practice.

JACK STALLINGS

The most important lesson we teach our players is as long as we compete the very best we can, as long as we go into a game prepared and give 100%, then we have to accept the outcome of the game.

SKIP BERTMAN

THE MOST VALUABLE THING YOU CAN GIVE
TO YOUR TEAM IS A GOOD EXAMPLE.

The only thing that's certain is that
the National Anthem is played before every game.

RICK MONDAY

The purpose of human life is to serve, to show compassion,
and the will to help others.

ALBERT SCHWEITZER

The right mental attitude makes such a difference in the game of baseball; keep your players in the best frame of mind at all times, so they are able to play to the best of their physical and mental abilities.

RICK WOLFF

The quality of a person's life is in direct proportion to their commitment to excellence regardless of their chosen field of endeavor.

VINCE LOMBARDI

There are three types of players: bulldogs, puppy dogs, and hot dogs.

DANNY DAVIS

There are 26 ways to score from third base. Get there!
GORDIE GILLESPIE

There are two basic ingredients in building rapport with your players.
First you have to establish it and then you have to keep it going.
RICK WOLFF

There's a subtle danger that a coach must avoid: fostering an attitude of
complete concentration on baseball. It would be tragic to allow an athlete to
become so narrow in his life's philosophy that baseball was all he lived for.
JERRY KINDALL

41

THERE IS A THIN LINE BETWEEN DISCIPLINE AND HARASSMENT. DISCIPLINE BREEDS SUCCESS. HARASSMENT BREEDS CONTEMPT.

There's nothing a baseball coach hates more than walks and dandelions.
CRAIG RUTTER

To win in baseball, you must
1. Throw strikes
2. Put the ball in play
3. Play catch
4. Have team spirit
5. Know the rules
6. Run the bases intelligently

WALLY KINCAID AND JOHN HERBOLD

Try not to become a man of success but rather try to become a man of value.

ALBERT EINSTEIN

Well, you can't win them all.
CONNIE MACK AFTER HIS 1916 PHILADELPHIA A'S WENT 36-117

What affects everyone can best be solved by everyone.

What you spent years building, someone could
attempt to destroy overnight. Build anyway.

When building a team, I always search first for people who love to win.
When I run out of those, I look for people who hate to lose.
ROSS PEROT

When I have learned all I need to make a decision,
I don't take a vote. I make a decision.
RONALD REAGAN

When you lose, don't lose the team.

When you realize you have made a mistake, take immediate steps to correct it.

When you study the great coaches, you see the one major trait that they all have in common - communication. They can communicate fully and directly with their team.
RICK WOLFF

Where there is no vision, the people perish.
PROVERBS 29:18

You can get everything in life you want
if you help enough other people get what they want.
ZIG ZIGLAR

You can motivate dedicated players, and players who believe in you,
your program and their teammates. You cannot
motivate players who feel no sense of responsibility or commitment to
you, your program, or their teammates.
WILLIAM WARREN

46

WHILE RADAR GUNS ARE VALUABLE AS A TOOL FOR MEASUREMENT AND FOR REFERENCE, A TEAM'S EVALUATIONS ARE MISGUIDED IF THEY USE THE READINGS AS THE DEFINITIVE MEASUREMENT OF A PITCHER. A RADAR GUN CAN'T TELL WHETHER A PITCHER HAS MASTERED THE ART OF PITCHING - THE LOCATION OF THE PITCHES, THEIR SEQUENCE, AND THEIR MOVEMENT IN THE HITTING ZONE.

Syd Thrift (Former General Manager of the Pirates/Yankees)

You can't let yourself get on that emotional roller coaster ride over wins and losses. You have to keep an even level of intensity, because there are so many variables in this game.

STEVE CARLTON

You cannot make a ballplayer out of somebody.
You can only give them an opportunity to make theirself into a player.

E.A.F. ANDERSON (CHARLIE GREENE'S HIGH SCHOOL COACH)

You have not lived today until you have done something for someone who can never repay you.

JOHN BUNYAN

You have to believe in yourself before others can believe in you.
TOMMY LASORDA

You're never as good as you look when you're winning, and you're never as bad as you look when you're losing.
EARL WEAVER

Your influence as a coach is an ever increasing shadow.
CARROLL LAND

YOUR TONGUE CAN DESTROY OR BUILD, TEAR UP OR MEND. USE YOUR WORDS TO BUILD CONFIDENCE IN YOUR TEAM.

Van Crouch

FOR THE PLAYER

"Motivation is something nobody else can give you. Others can help motivate you, but basically it must come from you and it must be a constant desire to do your very best at all times and under any circumstances."

JOE DIMAGGIO

A baseball swing is a finely tuned instrument developed through repetition, repetition, and more repetition.

REGGIE JACKSON

Ability is what you're capable of doing. Motivation determines what you do. Attitude determines how well you do it.

LOU HOLTZ

After having a minor league coach, who was a former major league catcher, set a pitching machine to throw up to 100 balls at a time in the dirt, Lance Parrish said: "It wasn't any fun, but believe me, it made me a much better catcher."

A goal, no matter how lofty, specific, or realistic, is worthless unless there is a commitment along with it, because goals without commitment are wasted.

JACK STALLINGS

A great hitter isn't born, he's made. He's made out of practice, fault correction, and confidence.

ROGERS HORNSBY

A hitter's impatience is the pitcher's biggest advantage.

PETE ROSE

All great hitters do the basic fundamentals very well in the lead-up procedures and sequences to the actual swing of the bat.

BEN HINES

Always do more than is required of you.

GENERAL GEORGE S. PATTON

A man rarely succeeds at anything unless he has fun doing it.

An athlete is not crowned unless he competes according to the rules.
I TIMOTHY 2:5

An outfielder who throws behind the runner is
locking the barn after the horse was stolen.
JOE McCARTHY

A pitcher who has superior ability but is obvious and predictable
will be less effective than one with modest ability but who
keeps the batter guessing.
PAT JORDAN

A player's greatest crippler. . . . . fear.
A player's greatest mistake. . . . . giving up.
A player's greatest loss. . . . . self-confidence.
A player's most potent force. . . . . positive thinking.

A player's individual success should be secondary
to the team concept of baseball.

JOE MORGAN

Are you worried about a pitcher's breaking or off-speed pitches, or are
you anticipating the fast ball he has to throw for a strike?

DAVE ALTOPP

ASKING FOR HELP IS A STRENGTH, NOT A WEAKNESS.

ATTITUDES ARE CONTAGIOUS. IS YOURS WORTH CATCHING?

Associate with those who help you believe in yourself.
BROOKS ROBINSON

Attitudes are more important than facts.
KARL MENNINGER

Baseball is a game of time and distance. Use what you know
to gain an advantage in one or both of these factors.

BILL ARCE

Character is your behavior when no one is looking.

NORMAN SCHWARTZKOPF

CONCEIT IS A STRANGE DISEASE.
IT MAKES EVERYONE SICK EXCEPT THE ONE WHO HAS IT.

Confidence is probably the most important characteristic for
a player to possess, and for some the hardest to obtain.
BRAGG STOCKTON

Control doesn't mean throwing strikes.
It means throwing a pitch where you want.
JUAN MARICHAL

Constructive criticism is a kick in the pants with a soft-sole shoe.

Dedication: an enthusiastic willingness to accept, even look forward to, the long hours of practice, conditioning and preparation necessary for excellence.

Desire: the dynamic motivation behind every worthwhile purpose; it is the inspiration that keeps one's passion to compete burning.

Do not alibi on bad hops. Anybody can field the good ones.
JOE McCARTHY

Don't be afraid to fail.
Experience is just mistakes you won't make anymore.
JOE GARAGIOLA

Don't grumble because you don't have what you want;
be thankful you don't get what you deserve.

Don't let any team awe you.
LUKE APPLING

Don't let the pressure of the competition
outweigh the pleasure of the competition.
KIRK KELLEY

Don't let what you cannot do interfere with what you can do.
JOHN WOODEN

Do your best and forget the rest.
WALT ALSTON

Easy street is always a road to defeat.

Everybody has limits. You have to learn what your own limits are and deal with them accordingly.

NOLAN RYAN

EVERY GOOD PLAYER WHO GOT WHERE HE IS STARTED FROM WHERE HE WAS.

Failure is success if you learn from it.

MALCOMB FORBES

EVERY MORNING IN AFRICA, A GAZELLE WAKES UP. IT KNOWS IT MUST RUN FASTER THAN THE FASTEST LION OR IT WILL BE KILLED. EVERY MORNING A LION WAKES UP. IT KNOWS IT MUST OUTRUN THE SLOWEST GAZELLE OR IT WILL STARVE TO DEATH. SO, IT DOESN'T MATTER WHETHER YOU ARE A LION OR A GAZELLE.

WHEN THE SUN COMES UP, YOU BETTER BE READY.

Every player should have goals.
They should be realistic and reflect improvement.

FALLING DOWN DOESN'T MAKE YOU A FAILURE,

BUT STAYING DOWN DOES.

Few athletes have the self-discipline to work to maximum when they
think that less than a maximum effort will suffice.

WILLIAM WARREN

For a batter to be physically ready to hit when he steps into the batter's box, requires that he must be mentally and overtly aggressive as a hitter. He must think that every pitch is going to be his pitch to hit.

BEN HINES

Give the world the best you have and it may never be enough. Give the world the best you've got anyway.

Giving myself wholeheartedly to workouts was no guarantee of success in the win-loss column. It did, however, rule out laziness and bad work habits as excuses.

OREL HERSHISER

Gordie Gillespie once asked Ted Williams "what he would do differently, if he could do it all over again?" Ted's reply: "I'd hit more."

Great pitchers don't allow trivial things to upset them.
ROGER CRAIG

Hitting a baseball is more mental than physical.
TY COBB

Hitting a baseball, I've said it a thousand times, is the single most difficult thing to do in sport.
TED WILLIAMS

Hitting is timing. Pitching is upsetting timing.
WARREN SPAHN

How you play the game shows something of your character.
How you lose shows all of it.

I couldn't wait to go to the ballpark. I hated it when we got rained out.
MICKEY MANTLE

I do the very best I know how, the very best I can, and I mean to keep on
doing so until the end.
ABRAHAM LINCOLN

I'd rather swing a bat than do anything else in the world.
TED WILLIAMS

If I can be an example as far as drugs are concerned,
my advice is to stay away from drugs and don't mess with them.
KEITH HERNANDEZ

IF MUSCLES WERE EVERYTHING, A BULL COULD CATCH A RABBIT.

If the human body recognized agony and frustration,
people would never run marathons, have babies, or play baseball.
CARLTON FISK

IF WHAT YOU DID YESTERDAY STILL LOOKS BIG TO YOU,

YOU HAVEN'T DONE MUCH TODAY.

If you can't outsmart people, outwork them.
BILL VEECK

If the team wins, we all had a good year.
If we don't win, then it doesn't matter who had a good year.

PAUL O'NEILL

If you have a will to win, you have achieved half your success;
if you don't, you have achieved half your failure.

DAVID AMBROSE

If you have class, you don't need much of anything else. If you don't have
it, no matter what else you have, it doesn't make much difference.

HOWARD FERGUSON

IF YOU STAND FOR NOTHING, YOU WILL FALL FOR ANYTHING.

I gave 110 percent to baseball out of sheer love for the game.
I asked no favors and gave none. I just concentrated on
playing the game hard every day.

ENOS SLAUGHTER

I never faced a pitcher that I didn't think I could hit.

PETE ROSE

I never blamed myself when I was in a slump; I blamed the bat and
if the slump continued, I changed bats. I know that sounds silly, but it
kept me from getting down in the dumps when I was in a slump.

YOGI BERRA

74

I have never encountered a successful athlete who claimed that drugs or alcohol enhanced their lives in any long-term sense. The smart ones, the truly self-assured ones, avoid them from the start. If you believe only one thing you hear from your parents, teachers, coaches, let it be this - don't do drugs! Don't abuse alcohol. Nobody's kidding you here. No one who cares about you would give you any other advice.

BOB COSTAS

IT DOESN'T TAKE ANY TALENT TO HUSTLE.

It has been said that there are two kinds of people:
those who do the work and those who take the credit.
Try to be in the first group; there is much less competition there.

I think the most important thing in life and in playing baseball is to try
and do the very best that you possibly can at all times.

HANK AARON

"I thought I raised a man, not a baby." What Mickey Mantle's dad said to him during his first year in the Yankee minor league system while he was suffering a major slump.

It is essential that you play with emotion without displaying emotion.

LARRY GIANGRASSO

It is much more important to develop good hitting mechanics and master the skill of making contact with the ball than to be concerned with how far the ball travels when you hit it.

CHARLIE LAU

It is virtually impossible to become an outstanding baseball player without learning to sacrifice somewhere along the way (going much beyond learning how to sacrifice bunt). A player must sacrifice time that would be spent doing other things, sacrifice his personal agenda to abide by team rules, make the sacrifices necessary to get along with the coach(es) and teammates, and accept the personal sacrifices involved with learning to function as a team rather than as an individual.

WILLIAM WARREN

It is not what men say about you that really matters.
It is what you believe about yourself.

It is your attitude, not your aptitude,
that will be the chief determinant of your success.

It's not the size of the bat. It's what you do with it.
TONY GWYNN

It's not the size of the dog in the fight. It's the size of the fight in the dog.

IT'S NOT WHAT HAPPENS TO YOU THAT COUNTS, BUT HOW YOU RESPOND.

It's tough to beat the person who never gives up.

BABE RUTH

I want to be remembered as a player who gave all he had to give.

ROBERTO CLEMENTE

I worked hard. I tried to take care of my body.
I wanted to never look back and say that I could have done more.
CARL YASTRZEMSKI

Keep your head up and you may not have to keep it down.
JOE MCCARTHY

Laying the blame for poor performance at the feet of the coach,
another player or an official is the universal cop-out and is practiced
daily by immature athletes all over the world.
NORM WILHELMI

LEARN FROM OTHER'S MISTAKES RATHER THAN MAKING THEM ALL YOURSELF.

Luck: a loser's excuse for a winner's position.

Man is the only creature who can reshape and remold himself by altering his attitude.

Man who said it cannot be done should not interrupt man doing it.
CHINESE PROVERB

Maturity: being big enough to say, "I was wrong," or "It was my fault," or "I am the one to blame."

Most of your tomorrows depend upon today.
ANDY LOPEZ

NEVER LOOK BACK UNLESS YOU WANT TO GO THAT WAY.

Never let the fear of striking out get in your way.
BABE RUTH

Never, never, never, never give up.
WINSTON CHURCHILL

Nobody ever became a ballplayer by walking after a ball.
JOE McCARTHY

No one can be truly successful by doing only what is required of them. Reaching a little higher is the amount of effort over and above the required that determines true excellence.
SKIP BERTMAN

No one can make you feel inferior without your permission.
No price is too high to pay for a good reputation.
Nothing is more common than unsuccessful men with talent.
Nothing will stop a hitter as quickly as fear and tension at the plate.

CHARLIE LAU

Others can stop you temporarily,
but you're the only one who can do it permanently.

JOHN MAXWELL

One of the beautiful things about baseball is that every once in a
while you come into a situation where you want to, and where
you have to, reach down and prove something.

NOLAN RYAN

People who have attained things worth having in this world have worked while others have idled, have persevered when others gave up in despair.

GRENVILLE KLEISER

People who never do any more than they get paid for,
never get paid for any more than they do.

Play every game as hard as you can, as aggressively as you can. Make that second effort on every play. You can't worry about the next play or tomorrow because you don't know what they may bring.

TY COBB

Players must learn to run the **RACE**.

Respect

Attitude

Commitment

Effort

SCOTT BERRY

Practice the game the way you're going to play the game.
Practice hard, play hard, and run hard. Above all else, hustle every
moment you're on the field whether it's practice or a game.

PETE ROSE

Profanity has never made a man out of a boy. The fact is that it is a crutch for those who are inferior conversationalists.

Quitting is a permanent solution to a temporary problem.

Regarding the "art" of pitching, Ray Miller (former major league pitching coach) said: "work fast, change speeds, throw strikes."

Rejoice in our sufferings, because we know that suffering produces perseverance, perseverance produces character, character brings hope, and hope does not disappoint us.
ROMANS 5:3-5

REMEMBER THAT GREAT ACHIEVEMENTS INVOLVE GREAT RISKS.

Remember the three R's:
Respect for self; Respect for others; Responsibility for all your actions.

Show me a guy who's afraid to look bad,
and I'll show you a guy you can beat every time.
LOU BROCK

S ince individual production cannot be completely controlled due to an unlimited number of variables (the actions of teammates, opponents, the direction of the wind, condition of the field, etc.), a player should focus on the things he can control, and players can control performance. Performance means the manner in which a skill is executed, *without regard to the outcome*. It is hitting the ball hard, throwing a good pitch, hustling and doing what can be controlled in the best way possible.

JACK STALLINGS

SOME OF THE "BEST," "GREATEST," AND "MOST."

The best day. . . . . today.
The greatest mistake. . . . . giving up.
The greatest need. . . . . common sense.
The most dangerous person. . . . a liar.
The most disagreeable person. . . the complainer.
The best teacher. . . . . one who makes you want to learn
The greatest victory. . . . . victory over self.

Some people have said to me that I am the most competitive person they have ever known. It's my passion for the game that makes me that way.

DON MATTINGLY

Some people make things happen and some wait for things to happen.
Then there are those who say, "What happened?"

Some pitchers want to be known as the fastest thrower that ever lived.
Some want to win 30 games in one season. Some want to pitch a no-hitter.
All I wanted was to be the best I could be, day after day.
TOM SEAVER

Some things in life you just can't buy - like great memories.
DON DRYSDALE

Speed is a bad qualification for pitching unless accuracy goes with it.
CY YOUNG

Stride, decide, then hit it hard.
JIM PIZZOLATTO

SUCCESS IS BEST MEASURED BY HOW FAR YOU HAVE COME WITH THE TALENTS YOU HAVE BEEN GIVEN.

Success is not measured by money or fame, but by how you feel about your own goals and accomplishments and the time and effort you put into them.
WILLIE STARGELL

Talent is God given - Be thankful
Fame is man given - Be humble
Conceit is self given - Be careful

The best thing about baseball is that you can do something
about yesterday tomorrow.

The depth of your commitment will be
reflected in the quality of your performance.

The difference between the possible
and the impossible lies in a person's determination.

TOMMY LASORDA

The fast ball is the only pitch that can't be taught.
You either have it or you don't.

JUAN MARICHAL

The first thing any pitcher *must* develop is control.

BABE RUTH

The fundamentals are the most valuable tools a player can possess.
DICK WILLIAMS

The goal of every at bat is to have a productive swing. A productive swing is one which produces a batted ball that is hard to defend.
MIKE SCHMIDT

The good you do today, people will often forget tomorrow.
Do good anyway.

The greatest teacher is visualization.
You see others do it, and you aspire to reach that level.
TONY KUBEK

The harder you work, the harder it is to surrender.
VINCE LOMBARDI

The key to pitching success lies in the pitcher's ability
to throw the ball on a downward plane.
BOB SHAW

The longer I live, the more I realize the impact of attitude on life. I am convinced that life is 10% what happens to me and 90% how I react to it. We are in charge of our attitudes.

CHARLES SWINDOLL

The one thing that players can most easily control that leads to successful performance are their work habits.

JACK STALLINGS

The most important person any player should work to be as good as is himself. Your first responsibility is to be the best you can be. There's nobody else like you, so why try to be like somebody else?

FRANK ROBINSON

The most important things in life are good friends and a strong bullpen.
BOB LEMON

THE PITCHER HAS ONLY GOT A BALL. I'VE GOT A BAT.
Hank Aaron

The player who never makes a mistake
is the player who never does anything.
HUGH JENNINGS

There is absolutely no way you can succeed
and take drugs at the same time. I don't care who you are.
ANDY VANSLYKE

There is a vast difference between disappointment and discouragement.
Disappointment is momentary and will soon past. Discouragement
weighs like a heavy burden on our minds.
It's OK to be disappointed, but work hard to avoid being discouraged.
JERRY KINDALL

There are three things I emphasize to any hitter before even considering the fundamentals of a good swing:

1) Proper thinking when stepping into the box
2) Get a good ball to hit
3) Be quick with the bat

TED WILLIAMS

There is no easy road to becoming a baseball pitcher. It is a road of self-denial, hard work, constant practice, ambition to improve, and an insatiable desire to do everything possible to become the best.

BOB SHAW

There is nothing owed to you.

BILL VEECK

The pitcher has to throw a strike sooner or later, so why not hit the pitch you want to hit and not the one he wants you to hit?

JOHNNY MIZE

The road to success is always under construction.

JIM DIMICK

THE TROUBLE WITH MOST PLAYERS IS THAT THEY WOULD RATHER BE RUINED BY PRAISE THAN SAVED BY CRITICISM.

The winners in life think constantly in terms of I can, I will, and I am. Losers, on the other hand, concentrate their waking thoughts on what they should have or would have done, or what they can't do.

DENNIS WAITLEY

**THINGS TURN OUT BEST FOR THOSE
WHO MAKE THE BEST OF THE WAY THINGS TURN OUT.**

Throw strikes! The plate don't move.
SATCHEL PAIGE

To get playing time you usually have to push someone ahead of you. It also helps to be pushed by someone behind you.

Though baseball is a team sport, each play is one on one:
man against man or man against the ball.
It's what you do individually that contributes to the team.

DAVE DRAVECKY

To get the most out of your ability, always work on your weaknesses.

JOE MORGAN

To know what is right and not do it is the worst cowardice.

CONFUCIUS

What counts is not the number of hours you put in,
but how much you put in the hours.

Whatever the game situation, the batter must always bring
a plan of attack to the plate. He should ask himself,
"what am I looking to accomplish in this at-bat?"
SYD THRIFT (FORMER GENERAL MANAGER FOR THE PIRATES/YANKEES)

What you are is God's gift to you.
What you make of yourself is your gift to God.

When an archer misses the mark, he turns and looks for the fault within himself. Failure to hit the bulls-eye is *never* the fault of the target. To improve your aim, improve yourself.

When asked how does he pitch to Hank Aaron, Don Newcombe replied, "I wish I could throw the ball under the plate."

When I played, I never thought of records, or personal statistics. I just tried to do all I possibly could to help my team win.

ROY CAMPANELLA

When I went out for my college baseball team, I couldn't get the coach to notice me, to give me a chance to bat. All he had me doing was chasing fly balls and after running around all afternoon in that hot Louisiana sun, I fell from exhaustion. After I came to and rested a little, the coach let me hit sort of as a goodwill gesture. I took five swings and hit four out of the park. Then they asked me my name and where I was from.

LOU BROCK

When the One Great Scorer comes to mark against your name, He writes - not that you won or lost - but how you played the game.

GRANTLAND RICE

When you're through learning, you're through.

VERNON LAW

Whether you're a little leaguer or a major leaguer, if you want to be a good hitter, you must first thoroughly understand the fundamentals and mechanics of hitting.

JERRY KINDALL

With two strikes your approach to hitting changes, but taking a third strike is a mortal sin. Dare the pitcher to throw a ball you cannot touch.

BUD DANIEL

Work! Work! Work! When you're tired, work some more. It is a matter of will. A player must have the will to get better every day.

GORDIE GILLESPIE

You are where you are and what you are because of the dominating thoughts that occupy your mind.

You can always pitch better.
SANDY KOUFAX

You can always take what you have and make it better.
TED WILLIAMS

You can have mechanics with no strategy,
but without mechanics, there is no strategy.
OREL HERSHISER

You cannot obtain success in baseball on the installment plan.
It must be paid for in advance.
GLEN TUCKETT

**YOU CAN'T HOOT WITH THE OWLS AT NIGHT
AND FLY WITH THE EAGLES DURING THE DAY.**

You can't win with potential; you can only win on performance.
SKIP BERTMAN

You don't break a bad habit by sitting back and hoping it will change.
You get your nose down in there and work at changing.
My college coach (Charlie Sarver) emphasized repetition and breaking
bad habits, two things I really needed at the time.

TODD WORRELL

You have the greatest chance of winning when your first commitment is
to a total and enthusiastic involvement in the game itself.

JOHN BRODIE

You have to get your uniform dirty.
PETE ROSE

**YOU NEVER GET AHEAD OF ANYONE AS
LONG AS YOU TRY TO GET EVEN WITH THEM.**

You never get a second chance to make a good first impression.

You'd be surprised how many shortcomings you overcome by hustle.
PETE ROSE

You never have to wait long or look far to be reminded of how thin the line is between being a hero or a goat.
MICKEY MANTLE

YOUR ATTITUDE SPEAKS SO LOUDLY THAT I CAN'T HEAR WHAT YOU SAY.

Your companions are like the buttons on an elevator.
They will either take you up or take you down.

You should have nothing on your mind when
you step into the batter's box *except* baseball.
PETE ROSE

You will never correct what you are unwilling to confront.

CLOSING THOUGHTS

S ome things are best said through poetry or prose. Here follows a few
of the better ones I have used over the years.

BASEBALL AND LIFE

by Bob Bennett

Baseball, like life
teaches us to endure,
but its false illusions
may also allure.

Success is offered
and failure too,
but commitment and effort
will usually shine through.

Sometime it is generous
and kind as well,
but often it is stingy
with hardships to sell.

Teamwork and honor
are its beacons of light,
but selfish persuasions
are often in sight.

Enjoyment and pleasure
are there to make,
but disappointment and heartbreak
are also at stake.

So take part in it
or let it pass by.
Lessons in baseball
to life they apply.

Bob Bennett has been the head baseball coach at Fresno State University in California for nearly 30 years. He has written a wonderful collection of poems about baseball and published them in a book entitled, *Words and Rhythms of Baseball* (1996).

GIVE YOUR BEST
by Bob Bennett

Commit to excellence
before you start.
Play each game
with all your heart.

To do otherwise
is to commit a ruse.
It puts your talent
to its poorest use.

The fullest feelings
you will possess,
when true commitment
you confess.

No more emptiness
from halfhearted tries.
Only your best
now applies.

You will not regret
this serious vow.
A winning look
is on your brow.

Positive Thinking

IF YOU THINK YOU ARE BEATEN, YOU ARE.
IF YOU THINK YOU DARE NOT, YOU DON'T.
IF YOU'D LIKE TO WIN BUT THINK YOU CAN'T,
IT'S ALMOST CERTAIN YOU WON'T.
LIFE'S BATTLES DON'T ALWAYS GO
TO THE STRONGER OR FASTEST MAN,
BUT SOONER OR LATER, THE MAN WHO WINS
IS THE MAN WHO THINKS HE CAN.

SERMONS WE SEE
by Edgar A. Guest

I'd rather see a sermon
than hear one any day.
I'd rather someone take my hand
than merely point the way.

For the eye's a better pupil,
more observant than the ear.
Fine counsel is confusing,
but example's always clear.

And the best of all our preachers
are the ones who live their creeds.
'Cause it's seeing good in action
that most everybody needs.

I soon can learn to do it -
if you'll let me see it done.
I can watch your hands in action,
but your tongue too fast may run.

And the lecture you deliver may be
very wise and true.
But I'd rather get my lessons
by observing what you do.

I might misunderstand
some of the high advice you give,
But there's no misunderstanding
how you act and how you live.

HOW TO TELL A WINNER FROM A LOSER
by Sydney J. Harris

A winner says, "let's find out."
A loser says, "nobody knows."

When a winner makes a mistake, he says, "I was wrong."
When a loser makes a mistake, he says, "it wasn't my fault."

A winner credits his "good luck" for winning, even though it wasn't good luck.
A loser blames his "bad luck" for losing, even though it wasn't bad luck.

A winner knows how and when to say "yes and no."
A loser says, "yes, but" and "perhaps not" at the wrong times, for the wrong reasons.

A winner paces himself.
A loser has only two speeds, hysterical and lethargic.

A winner works harder than a loser and has more time.
A loser is always "too busy" to do what is necessary.

A winner goes through a problem.
A loser goes around it and never gets past it.

A winner makes commitments.
A loser makes promises.

A winner says he's sorry by making up for it.
A loser says, "I'm sorry," but does the same thing the next time.

A winner knows what to fight for and what to compromise on.
A loser compromises on whxat he shouldn't and fights for what isn't worth fighting about.

A winner listens.
A loser just waits until it's his turn to talk.

A winner respects those who are superior to him and tries to learn something from them.
A loser resents those who are superior to him and tries to find chinks in their armor.

A winner feels responsible for more than his job.
A loser say, "I only work here."

A winner says, "there are ought to be a better way to do it."
A loser says, "that's the way it's always been done around here."

A winner has a healthy appreciation of his abilities, and a keen awareness of his limitations.
A loser is oblivious both of his true abilities and his true limitations.

A winner judges himself by the standard of excellence in his field.
A loser judges himself by the standard of mediocrity in his field.

A winner is sensitive to the atmosphere around him.
A loser is sensitive only to his own feelings.

A loser blames "politics" or "favoritism" for his failure.
A winner would rather blame himself than others when he falls short.

A loser feels cheated if he gives more than he gets.
A winner feels that he is simply building up credit for the future.

A loser is envious of winners and contemptuous of other losers.
A winner judges others only by how well they live up to their own capacities, not by some external scale of worldly success.

A loser says, "it can't be done."
A winner says, "all things are possible."

THE INDISPENSABLE MAN

Sometime when you're feeling important,
Sometime when your ego's in bloom,
Sometime when you take it for granted,
You're the best qualified in the room.

Sometime when you feel that your going
Would leave an unfillable hole,
Just follow these simple instructions
And see how it humbles your soul.

Take a bucket and fill it with water.
Put your hand in it up to the wrist,
Pull it out and the hole that's remaining
Is the measure of how you'll be missed.

You may splash all you please when you enter.
You may stir up the water galore,
But stop and you'll find in a minute
That it looks just the same as before.

The moral of this quaint example
Is do just the best that you can.
Be proud of yourself, but remember
There is no indispensable man.

WINNERS MAKE THE CHOICE:

To get something out of all situations, rather than complain about them.
To hustle, rather than dog it.
To be prepared, rather than occasionally.
To be early, rather than just on time - or late.
To want to learn, rather than want to explain or excuse.
To do more, rather than just enough - or less.
To be mentally tough, rather than mentally lazy or intimidated.
To concentrate on what to do, rather than what may result.
To be aggressive, rather than passive - or submissive.
To know their limitations, rather than try to do more than they are
are capable of.
To think about solutions, rather than worry about problems.
To accept adversity as part of life, rather than magnify the adverse
conditions and seek sympathy.
To think and act positively, rather than negatively.

SOME THINGS NEVER CHANGE
by Bob Bennett

Some things never change,
they simply stay the same.
Dignity and class
hold this claim.

True friendship and love
are as constant as air.
They hold together
in times of despair.

Honor and trust
stay the course.
They do not waiver
from power or force.

Integrity is inflexible.
Its definition is always the same.
It does not falter
in the heat of the game.

Plans and goals
we may rearrange,
but these values
never change.

The leaves on a tree
will change with the season,
but some things never change
no matter the reason.